Embracing *the* Diamond Within

NO PRESSURE, NO DIAMOND

Angela Elder

ISBN 979-8-89043-587-3 (paperback)
ISBN 979-8-89043-586-6 (digital)

Christian Faith Publishing
832 Park Avenue
Meadville, PA 16335
www.christianfaithpublishing.com

Printed in the United States of America

To my Lord and Savior
Thank you for your grace and mercy

To My Daughters
Who gave me unconditional Love and believed
in me even when I did not believe in myself.

To My Husband
Thank you for loving me and just letting me be me.

INTRODUCTION

This book is not about the shame of life's journey. It is not about putting people in the spotlight, but rather, it is about the healing journey of all our decisions and actions and the effect on us from other people's decisions and actions.

This is about stepping into your truth. I used my case in the chapters so that you will know that you're not alone. Take a challenge just as I did and go for what you want, for in Jesus's name, you shall succeed. It is time to release the pressure and reveal the diamond God created.

CONTENTS

CHAPTER 1

The Search for the Diamond

When you search for something, even if you do not know what it is you are searching for, be prepared to accept the finding. Set your mind on the fact that we all have a story in our heads, but God has the original story He set for you before you were born. We and everyone we have come in contact with have changed the direction of our story, but may God's will be done if you just release. You may think that there's no exciting thing happening in your life, but I assure you there will be a change if you take a challenge. The will of God can only be done if you take challenges, so take challenges until things begin to change.

Don't think that the search is easy because good things cannot be found easily. But as the Bible says in Jeremiah 29:11–14 (NIV),

> "For I know the plans I have for you." Declares the Lord, "plan to prosper you plans to give and not to harm you, plans to give you hope and a future. Then you will call on me and come and pray to me, ad I will listen to you. You will seek me and find me when you seek me with all you heart. I will be found by you," declares the LORD, "and will bring you back from captivity."

You just have to get to the point in your life that you believe what the word says. I have always been drawn to this scripture, but it took years for me to truly believe that it was for me.

Inside perspective

Sometimes you have to ask yourself, "Who am I now?" just to reason about your journey from an inside perspective. In this regard, I have my five personal answers to who I am now.

First. I am the daughter of the Highest. He loves me unconditionally. His love for me is something that you cannot explain. It is a love that makes you feel at peace with your life. A love that helped you move from your past to your future with no hurdles. But at times, it has been a love that caused me confusion. Yes, I do be confused about how I can be loved so much by someone I haven't seen, after the things I've done, and after all the rejections received in my life and all the rejections I've exhibited toward Him. God is a mystery, but a mystery that can be solved. His love is unconditional, and He gives you the space to discover all the mysteries if you're obedient to the gospel. Or should I say it's not a mystery? God is clear if you want to hear Him. God is there if you want to be with Him. He loves you. When you don't want to be loved, He holds you when you don't want to be held. He's always in reach when you're ready. So that's why I can proudly say now I am a daughter of the Most High, although it has been a journey that I will discuss as we continue. Do understand it is not an easy one but a journey well worth traveling to find myself and to know without a doubt whose I am and who I continue to develop into by grace.

Second. I am who I am, and I choose to accept myself. I cannot be anyone else. God created me be me to bring glory to him. Yes, I have been abused, talked about, disrespected, and hurt, but God has been faithful to me even when I could not feel His presence. It has taken years to accept myself, nevertheless worrying about others accepting me. I realized that people will always find something wrong with you, and they have no issue bringing to light all your faults in this life journey. This affects me now; this is something that has delayed me from even doing what God has advised me to do. People, people can keep you away from your God-given gift. People, humanity makes you feel worthless, but God does not make anything that is worthless, and that is probably one of the hardest lessons of life that I had to learn. People will talk about you in your face and even behind your back. People will say they love you but will be doing things that harm you. Because most of the time, when someone is hurting you, it is because they live a life of confusion and are unaware of how unsettling they can be to others. Or let us just say it in another way; some people enjoy making others feel worthless. So if anybody makes you feel worthless, that is because you already feel worthless within yourself, so I had to take the journey of believing in who I am, what I'm created to do, and mainly being myself and accepting myself. Just as you can see, the name of *I am* is how God chose to introduce Himself, becoming so sacred that the name is not to be spoken in Judaism. The significance of God's self-given name encompasses all that He is and how we are to relate to Him. God has also given you a name, and that is who you are so believe it when you say I am who I am because God created me to be.

Third. I am a wife for the third time. First two marriages, I failed. Boy, did I fail because I did not know who I was? I failed because I was something for someone else that I was not for myself. But it was God's plan for me to be a wife to my current husband at this time in my life and in his life. The time when God said, "I am here, and now it is time for you to get up, show up, and be what I designed you to be, so get up and walk in your destiny." I had to push back the feeling of failure just to move forward in God's plan for my life. Someone told me one time that you should never be divorced because it's a sin in God's eyes. I let that statement dictate that I was not wor-thy of a wonderful relationship because I had failed myself and God. But I also believe the Bible, which states in Matthew 9:6 (NIV), "So they are no longer two, but one flesh. Therefore what God has joined together, let no one separate." So the reality was God did not put those marriages together, and that is why they failed. And to be honest, failure is not always bad. Failing at something only gives you a reason to stop and ask God for His assistance because without God, you continue to set yourself up for failure. So I had to stop and examine myself and put in the time and energy to understand the choices I made and how it affected me and others. I had to hit the bottom in reference to relationships to understand that until I had a relationship with my Creator, I truly could not compete, and I would continue to fail.

Fourth. I am most proud of being a mother to two wonderful young women. Was it easy? No. Did I make mistakes? Yes, in massive ways. But God planned them for me and me for them. We are strong women who believe in always doing our best, being our best, and loving others to bring out the best in them. But I made so many mistakes when it came to my daughters. I was so broken and didn't know I was that broken because I was one of those people that had it all together. People would see me and think I had it all and was always at my best. I lived a life where I lacked nothing, but behind what they saw was just a woman who lacked a true understanding of who she was. Now who are you? Are you a mother of how many, and how are you impacting them? Don't allow your mistakes to limit you and don't place yourself where you are not always pursuing what is right.

Fifth. I am now married to a pastor—again, that was God's plan, and, boy, was it a wild one. This was something that I never saw coming, nor was I looking for it. I just wanted to be a child of God and be on a level that I could understand. I wanted someone in my life that just loved me for me. No adjustments needed.

However, I found out that to be a true child of God, you must be taken out of your understanding and comfort zone and sometimes, like me, be taken out of your current life and be placed in the unknown so that God can be seen in you.

Because God had a plan, and I faithfully stepped out in 2014 to get married after knowing my husband for seven months, and moving to be with my new husband, most people thought I was crazy; and honestly it was a little crazy. But God, in his small voice, said to me, "It will be okay." So all I could say to family, friends, and whoever asked was I know I have to go and marry him. I began to fulfill God's plan for my life. I realized that He selected me to be transparent by telling my story.

Not everyone will understand; they will judge me for my past, but my God has spoken to me, and I am here to be obedient to His plans for me.

Therefore, I do not need you to qualify me to be where I am, which was extremely hard for me, but I had to realize God has chosen me to be here at this time. God created me and my destiny. I no longer worry about where people seem to have placed me because God has prepared and qualified me for this story. He has used my failures, disobedient behaviors, and my fears to get me to the point I am at.

So it is time to put on my robe and tell the story of how I made it over. What you call disappointment, God calls preparation of the anointing. You do not pick your assignment, you have to give in to it and walk because God will guide you. It is not an easy matter, it will be one of the hardest things you will ever do because walking into God's purpose for you is not always clear and simple. It does not come with directions, it comes with daily guidance that you have to continue to be in prayer about what you are doing because as you continue to walk in your purpose, the devil continues to distract you. Yes, you will be distracted and sometimes take the wrong turn, letting fear, people's opinions, and daily messes make you feel that you are not made for this.

It makes you question what you are doing, "Is this really God's plan for me?" The main thing is to keep listening to God's voice because He brought you to the point, and He will continue to guide you to the finish line. Just hold on and keep walking. You will trip, you may look back and cry, and you will fall but do not try to run. Take your time move one step at a time and feel God's presence on your journey and keep walking into your purpose.

CHAPTER 2

Unexpected Brokenness

Brokenness, think about it if humanity wasn't broken, God would not have ever had to send Jesus down to die for our sins. The one thing about brokenness that makes it difficult for us is that we always think we're the only broken ones. Everyone in this world has come to the point of being broken. It's about "Are you ready to heal, are you ready to forgive, and are you ready to love when people are not lovable?"

Another way of seeing brokenness is seeing it as an opportunity to become deeper in awareness of who God is and seeing it as being able to come closer to God through your brokenness. And also, remember that in God's eyes, there is no unexpected brokenness. He is totally aware of where you are in your life at all times. He has prepared a place in your soul in your being that's just for Him. So don't be upset about the brokenness. Search for the space for healing.

My brokenness, you don't have to have been raised in brokenness to be considered broken. I was raised in a home with what would be called a whole family. My parents loved each other and showed love to my brother and me. But I was broken I didn't know. But what I did know is that something was missing.

I had what you would consider a good life. I lacked for nothing; I was given the best. I was considered a spoiled military brat because I was from a military family. We traveled and meet many types of people, but I was always alone. I always felt I was not good enough. People always wanted more from me. No one could just accept me for who I was, making me question myself. I could become what you say is a chameleon. I could change to be what people wanted me to be. I remember when I talked to black people, they would say you sound white. Therefore, I would never be black enough, and I would never be white so what the hell. People would always find a way to make me feel that I was just not enough.

I recall a situation that has stuck with me since I was twelve years old while visiting family for the summer in the South. As a young girl, I was expected to do certain chores, such as washing the dishes and sweeping the floor. These were not chores that were uncommon to me. But I was raised in a different environment that was not as accepted, so instead of understanding the difference, I was called lazy because it was not done to their standards. These were all ubiquitous things for a young lady, like washing dishes by hand and sweeping the entire house, except I was raised with a dishwasher in my home and wall-to-wall carpet. Therefore, I was not lazy; I was just raised in a different environment. My differences did not make me lazy or worthless, as some wanted me to believe, and I did believe.

It also makes me recall that during an argument, a family member took it upon themselves to, as I say, cut deep. They took it upon themselves to share some information that was considered a secret. Remember, when people cut, they subdue to their own insecurities not because it is something you have done, but because being angry with someone is a different cause when you do or say something that cuts so deep. Cutting deep is when you are truly trying to cause pain to someone that you cannot take back, and the pain can last years and be transferred from one generation to another. It is a pain that does not go away. They speak words that are so damaging that only God can heal. So in their anger, they dug deep and blurted out you were not supposed to be a part of this family anyway. You were put up for adoption.

As I froze and the words penetrated through my gut, I just wanted to bust them in the face, but the rage was held back due to the pain of the statement having pierced my heart for years. So now that it was out because someone heard the argument, now they wanted to tell the story. Yes, I was put up for adoption, and the new family was chosen, but my grandfather stopped the process, and my mother brought me home. This was something that made a crack in my core to the point I have not dealt with that family member ever again. I found out that day that people will destroy your entire being just to feel better about themselves. I never remembered what the argument was about; I only remember that day broke me, and forgiveness has been a long journey that I have not gotten to the end of it yet.

I have found that the journey is hard because when family secrets are involved, you get pieces of the truth when people are dying or angry, which is very difficult to handle. It is so funny that when people are dying, they want to tell the family secrets, but you will never get all the information because once they are gone, no one else seems to have any information, or they feel it is not their place to tell you. This is extremely hard because you are left with living a lie, and they rather keep a promise than help you find the truth, which leaves you in a whirlwind of anger, hurt, confusion, and disbelief. It crushed you to the point that you can't trust anyone. You are back to feeling unworthy, and people don't think enough of you to understand or care about the pain they have caused.

This pain was the cause of a lot of bad decisions. You spend your life trying to be there for people who make you feel that it would not matter to them whether you are in their life or not in their life. Or whether you live or die. It makes you search for love in the wrong places and settle for what people give you instead of what you deserve. Learning your worth is one of the hardest lessons you will ever learn.

Another important thing is learning that God loves you unconditionally, and there is nothing you can do to stop God's love for you. It just takes time to realize that kind of love believe in that love and trust in that love. It is not a physical love like you get from your parent, a child, or a man. It is a love that lives in your core. Just know that the hole in your heart will only be filled by knowing God's love for you.

CHAPTER 3

If the Reality Is with No Pressure, There Will Be No Diamond

This is the kind of pressure that will bring you to the floor. It will bring you to your knees where you honestly need to be. The pressure makes you feel like your life is twirling and whirling, you're spinning and spinning, and you can't gain control. Your emotions are on overload and underload; you're numb and weak. This pressure makes you wonder, why am I alive? Why Lord? This is the pressure that makes you who God created you to be:

- The pressure of the dream versus the truth
- The pressure that makes you feel unworthy

- The pressure that takes your soul and maybe your life
- The pressure of my reality versus spiritual truth

I will do a disclaimer on this part. This is not to hurt anyone, it's just to tell about God's grace. We are who we are now due to our past, but it's not about our past, it's about our future, and I am so much better of a woman or a human than I could ever have been if it wasn't for the past.

I am not sure where to start telling the story of this journey of truth versus the reality of my life. So let's start by saying forget the dream. Not saying dreams are bad, but before you get to the reality of your dreams, you have to go through the reality of life and piss poor decisions. Yes, I said pissed poor because some of that past decisions almost took me out emotionally, financially, spiritually, and if I am being truthful, those decisions almost caused me to lose my life. Life is hard, and it truly can make you or break you. God does give us the strength to maneuver through, but honestly, it took me a while to believe that. There were many days, nights, and years to get through my head, and God had my back. Therefore, I made such terrible decisions in my life regarding relationships, jobs, and money, and I did not believe in God's word. But if you read His word, it stands true, reflected in all of our lives. Well, the lack of understanding of God's word, I start my downward fall from grace. I got married for the first time.

Yes, I said the first time because I thought I needed what he had to give. He was an outgoing person life of the party. But on the day of my wedding, I felt the tug in my gut, saying this wasn't right. I continued with the wedding because I was committed and always stood by my word. Well, that marriage leads to lies, theft, and embarrassing actions. My husband was young, and he did the best he could with what he knew. This marriage took me on a journey where my credit was first abused. My husband opened up credit cards in my name at the time, and he wrote checks with my signature. You wonder how, well again, young and trusting. He would take the book of checks from the bottom of the box. From the book, he would write checks. At the time, I had no reason to balance my checkbook because I was aware of the check I was writing until the ones he wrote started to catch up. That is when the dream busted, and reality kicked in. Bank called about bounced checks, bad checks, and legal actions—what in the hell is going on? To only then find out that I am pregnant and had to declare bankruptcy. This in my eyes just could not be real.

Now life has thrown me a twist. I got legal problems that may cause me to lose my job. How could someone who said they love me do this? But now I am pregnant, and my pregnancy was a painful one. I was sick from the day I found out. To be exact, I went to the hospital because I could not hold down anything including water. The doctor said, "You are dehydrated, and you have a stomach virus when the test came back, but I cannot give you any medication because you are pregnant." I don't know about anyone else, but that is one heck of a way to find out that your life will change greatly, and that was the start of a long, dangerous pregnancy. So from that moment on, I was in a battle for my life. I say that because my marriage is pretty much over, and I am so sick that I end up in the hospital more times than I could count during the pregnancy.

The hospital stays continued for four and a half months. I continue to be admitted to the hospital for weeks at a time due to dehydration. It got to the point where I was fed from a tub in one arm and IVs and medication in the other. Until the time came when all my veins started to collapse, nurses were having a hard time being able to draw blood and continue with the feeding tub. Then the final night came when the nurse came in only to realize that the last vein I had cannot be used, so now she needed to call the doctor because he needed to choose to continue to feed me through the feeding tube or give me medicine because only one vain was still useful. This was a rough moment for the nurse and me because she had been my nurse from the beginning, trying to save me and my baby. I had become emotional for us both.

I had been seen by at least ten doctors giving experimental drugs to assist me in keeping food down and to prevent me and my baby from starving. I was at the stage where the doctors were saying they had never seen a pregnancy at this level of sickness. They were just at loss, and I was feeling like a guinea pig in a testing lab.

Then one Friday evening, the doctor came into my room to say. "There is nothing else we can do. Your veins are collapsing. We can no longer give you food or medicine. You and the baby are starving. If something does not happen in twenty-four hours to turn this around, we will have to conduct an abortion to save your life."

My reality of having a baby went out the window at that moment. I was pissed, and I had been sick for four and a half months in unbearable pain. I would not even discuss if it was a girl or boy and did not want to talk about names. I did not want to get so attached to the baby. I just wanted to stop being so sick. The smell of food sickened me. As a matter of fact, I could not even drink water without throwing up. How could I come this far to lose?

I remember my mother looking at me, saying that it is in God's hand now, and if I am being truthful, I was like, *What the hell is it that He let me go through all this, and now it is in His hands?* Mmmm, okay, I am still sick and pissed. But I was not crazy, so at this point, I had to call on the only help I knew. I had to call the name above all names, Jesus. It is the name I was taught but was not truly trusting in. But what did I have to lose? It was clear that my life and the life of my child were in danger. So as you can imagine, that was one long, long night, waiting for the twenty-four-hour mark to come. The thoughts that go through my head, the anger of being pregnant and not being able to enjoy it like other women, there was not a glow in me the was only sickness and pain, doctors and hospitals, and no one knows what is going on and why my body was rejecting this pregnancy.

As said in Psalms 30:5, "Weeping may endure for a night, but joy will cometh in the morning." But when the morning came, I was screaming in pain. The nurse came in, and they thought I was having a miscarriage but no. They called the doctor only for me to go into emergency surgery, and the doctor was like, "We have to do something," so they went in to find that the cyst that was making me sick because it did not decrease as it should have, instead it continued to grow and take all the nutrients from the feeding tube and had grown larger than the baby and was now moving and had twisted itself into a knot, which was causing the pain. So they removed the cyst along with my right ovary. When I came out of surgery, the doctor could only say that they didn't know if the pregnancy would hold. There is a fifty-fifty chance. I stayed in the hospital for another two weeks, only to leave weighing 103 pounds.

The doctor said to go home and eat anything I can eat because I need to gain weight. We were still not out of the woods yet. Sadly he was right. By the time I was ready to deliver, I had gone to a checkup appointment only to find out that I had toxemia and needed to deliver the baby within twenty-four hours, or we both could die. So fast track to delivery and deliver a beautiful baby girl. But she lacked oxygen, so while they had to give her oxygen, they also had to rush me to ICU. The baby was now fine, but I was still fighting for my life. I remained in ICU for five days.

During these five days, my husband at the time was nowhere around. That statement I had a praying momma was true. Then the devil was trying to kill my baby and me. He was also working overtime to destroy me mentally, financially, physically, and emotionally. He did accomplish some of the work because my marriage was gone, and my finances were gone. My husband was in the street with other women.

When I got out of ICU and was in a room, this man (boy) brought one of his women into my room to see the baby. That level of disrespect floored me. Someone who said he loved me would bring a woman to the hospital and wanted to let her hold my baby. The fact he thought it was okay is beyond my understanding, and the disrespect did not stop there. Even though bringing a woman to my hospital room was disrespectful, that was not the worst for me. The worst was when he called his friends and told them he was coming to my house to harm me. Only his friend would call to give me a heads-up. But I knew him enough to know he was just talking to be talking, but he came to visit the baby one day, and we got into a disagreement. When he was leaving, I went to give him a picture of his daughter. He snatched the picture from me and threw it on the ground. I recalled looking him straight in the face and saying, "You will never receive a picture of your daughter from me again." I have stood by that statement to this day.

Then as things continued, he started to threaten me, which led to me making a statement to him. The statement was, "I am trained to shoot a gun, and if you threaten me again, I will shoot you, and I am not trained to wound you." I was trained for a kill shot, and I will never serve a day in jail due to your continued threats. That was the last day he came by. So that also means he was never in my daughter's life. His lies, manipulation, and self-centeredness were not something I was going to have my daughter be a victim of. If he could not put her first, it was my job to protect her until she was ready to deal with him on her own or until he could truly be a father to her, which never happened.

So for me, let's just forget the dream because it is over. Not saying dreams are bad, just saying before you get to the reality of your dreams, you have to go through the reality of life.

Life is hard, and it truly can make you or break you. God does give us the strength to maneuver through, but honestly, it took me a while to believe that. There were many days, nights, and years to get through my head, and God had my back. Therefore, I made some terrible decisions in my life in relationships, jobs, and money, and most of all, I did not believe that God's word was for me. So I continue in a motion of disrespect and dishonor. Anger and pain will let you destroy yourself. Be aware God works on His time, not ours. I endured weeping for many days, months, and years before the joy came.

CHAPTER 4

The Pressure Makes You Feel Unworthy

God has made you worthy. That is all you need in your life because humanity will always try to make you feel unworthy. Satan wants to rule humanity, and people rather live worldly than live life differently. The children of God live a separate life from the world, but we all would stand to show the world that God has made them worthy.

Now this is hard to be in a position of feeling unworthy. At the time, I was now divorced, and I was a single mother working and trying to do my best when I was introduced to a lovely man. We worked in the same career, and he was very as nice and put together. He came from a good family, as we would say. He had a sister whom I became good friends with. As a matter of fact, his sister became my best friend. But reality kicked in, and it came with an exact vengeance. No matter how nice he was, he came with a very controlling, insecure mother. He was a momma boy, and that is not cute in any way. At first, I was like, who would not want to be with a man that loves his mother? But some levels are just unhealthy for any relationship, and in my experience, it was very unhealthy, and it cost me. The cost was a price that after twenty-plus years, I am still paying the price.

This relationship was the one where what his mother wanted was the way it was. In my eyes, she was very insecure to the point that she controlled most of her children. Sadly, she mainly had issues with other women. She had no respect for women in her son's life, and she had one daughter that she treated like a woman trying to destroy the relation-ship with her husband and son. She treated her in my eyes like she was an inconvenience and a threat instead of a daughter.

So as our relationship continued, it was obvi-ous that I was not welcome by his mother because I spoke my mind and had no intention of bowing down to her. She was a woman who attended church, but her use of the Bible made me see her as a witch with a Bible. I learned that insecure women with a Bible are walking beings of destruction, and they will use the Bible to destroy anything they fear. So you better know the word for yourself.

Even with all these clear in-my-face issues, I disregarded them, and we moved in together. Yes, we stacked up. And then I got pregnant and had my second daughter, and that is when the real mommy control kicked in. He was a good person and a good father, but he was a better son, and there was no way he would cut the cord.

As a matter of fact, it just got worse. We broke up, and that was when the true nasty came out. It was so bad that his sister, who at the time I considered my best friend, turned on me. You know the old saying, circle the wagon. Well, that is what his family did. Sadly it was only done to please the need of his mother. She failed so massively with her own daughter that she used her control over her son to get mine. She appeared to have such a desire to fix what she destroyed, which was her destruction of her own daughter, so they helped her destroy my relationship with my daughter because I was weak. I did not trust who I was. It is that old saying that hurting people hurt others. So in her pain and his desire to please his mother, he accused me of child abuse. This was something that just rocked me because everyone knew it was not true, but my so-called best friend sided with her family to get on her mother's good side.

After several court dates because we were in court every other month and the fact that he was not a bad person and I knew he loved his daughter and I had another child that I had to protect, I made a decision that changed my life, but for me, it was in a continuous spiral of shame. To stop the continuous court battles, I gave him custody of my daughter, and I remember that day and that pain like it just happened. The day I handed her over, I said to him, "You know everything you have said and done in court was a lie, and you are doing this for your mother. From this point, you will not see me again. I will not do visitation. You were willing to do anything to please your mother, so here, but understand your mother has an issue with women. Therefore, by the time she reaches thirteen years old and starts having her own opinion and voice, she will want to come and live with me."

Well, ten years later, that was what happened. I received a call from my daughter telling me that she wanted to come and live with me. Her father was fighting it. I had not spoken to him in ten years, and she asked me to call him. So I did, and the only thing I said was, "I told you this was going to happen. Your mother will never change, so let my daughter go."

A few weeks later, I went and picked her up. The most annoying part of that day was her grandmother, who had the nerve to be crying, and she stated to me, "Please don't keep her away from us." I disdained her when this woman took my child and accused me of horrible things. Kept my child from my family and me even when her cousins, my brother's daughters, lived across the street from them. This woman would not let my daughter have anything to do with them. But at that moment, all I could say was, "I won't do what you did to me."

But there was still a price to pay with my daughter and her pain of me not being there. I have to admit I let fear and anger let me decide, but now I have to deal with the consequences of that and understand her pain. She was angry, confused, and hurt, which has taken years to repair, and there is still work to do. But it is not the work you would expect. Because I am not asking for her to forgive me or to understand why. Some would say, "Why would you not ask for forgiveness?" Because in the matter, I do not want my daughter to feel obligated to forgive me because I asked for it. This is not something I can ask of her because the pain she feels from what she sees as me abandoning her is hers, and the healing that needs to be done is hers when she is ready. I had to do the work of forgiving myself for letting my fear of the possibility of child protection services into my home, the fear of the lies control my decisions, instead of trusting and knowing myself and my parenting. I felt that who would believe me when my best friend turned against me and sided with him? Fear can steal everything from you.

So now I just walk in faith, and the work continues toward healing on her terms and time. Because as we get older, we realize that forgiveness is nothing without healing. Healing is the main thing that is needed in our lives, and forgiveness will come. Pain and regret are just a direction to death, and I chose to live and heal with both of my daughters on their terms because my decision also stole a sister relationship from both of them, and that is a very large pill to take. But it is a pill I had to take straight with no chaser.

Because I know now my worth, I am clear now that during that season of my life, I was worthy, but I let fear control my actions. Fear ate at me like a parasite eating at me from the inside out. Even though I was angry at his mother for her controlling, lying behavior, it was not her fault. I was weak, and I let fear step in and take my daughter. I did not trust the court system, myself, and mainly I did not trust God. But fear is not of God.

CHAPTER 5

The Pressure Can Take Your Soul and Your Life

This pressure will leave you breathless. But with the love of God, He will always breathe life into you because you will need every breath just to feel, grow, and survive.

Pressure comes in so many ways. For me, it was relationships that gave me the most pressure. I always gave more than what was given. It was not their fault, it was mine. I had an uncanny ability to become what someone else needed and leave out what I needed. So when it got to the point in a relationship that I needed my needs to be met, it all fell apart because they were like, "You changed." When really the change was when I got into a relationship with them.

So now it is like, "I don't like you and do not have any true love for you. I don't need you any longer." How can I blame them? They were used to the person they unknowingly changed to fit their needs, and they liked that person. But when it was time for my needs to be met well, they did not sign up for that.

So as time continued, I entered into a new relationship and got married again. That was after three years of dating at the time, and it's a wonderful person that was about family. It is clear I am attracted to the so-called family man. But that can be an issue when they are so into their family that you have no true place. When the family-oriented person can blind people, they can sometimes look at the outside and become blinded by the inside. As I said, when it comes to relationships and family, sometimes the book cover is beautiful, but when you open the book, there is some piss poor reading, and for me, that was where my reality lay. It looked good from the outside, but when you can't keep up the show, it begins to crumb, and the light starts highlighting the faults. By our first anniversary, it was over.

I recall nothing for an anniversary gift, and for Christmas, my gift was two Hanes sweatsuits given to me in a Walmart bag. The verbal abuse started in such a manner that you were not speaking to but was spoken at and was called names such as bitch and told "you are so fat" even though I was in size 6 at the time. At this time, I only have my oldest daughter with me because my youngest daughter was living with her father due to the issue in my last relationship. The verbal statements were extreme, but I continued in public as there were no issues until public life met private life. I was working with a young lady that just looked up to me. She saw me as a strong, controlled, and independent woman. She was always like, "I want to be like you when I grow up."

Well, her husband did power washing, and we hired him to power wash our home. I told her it would be fine for her to come with him the day he came. I welcomed her into my home, which was made for me to have a guest, but because I never felt like it would be okay with him, I just never really had people he did not know come by. Only to find out my feeling we're right. After the visit, I went back to work. She came to my office and ask to close my door to speak to me.

When she sat down, she looked me straight in the face and said, "Who in the hell was that the other day?" That statement hit me in the gut because I knew my two lives had just collided, and I was sick.

The public life and the private life were drastically different from each other. Public life had us loving each other's wonderful household and wonderful couple working together to build a life. But my private life was full of put-downs and insults.

Then you are going on years of marriage when you notice that his pain from his so-called great family life was the reason for his abusive behavior. You realize that you were killing yourself by letting it continue. I recall the worst day was when we just left the accountant doing our taxes. I was driving home when he got angry, yelling at me from the passenger sit, calling me all kinds of names, and saying, "I can't take you anywhere! You embarrass me!" He then raised and came across close to my face and said, "You bitch."

At that point, I snapped and slammed on the brakes. The SUV that I was driving spun around in the street before coming to a stop in the other lane. Thankfully no cars were coming at that time. It was truly only by the grace of God that there was a space between me, the cars behind me, and the car in front that there was not an accident. Once, the car came to a stop. He was scared, and so was I. The fact that I did that or the fact I let his hate toward me caused me to put my life in danger. Well, that was the last straw. I filed for a divorce, and hell really showed up. A divorce that should have taken six months took two years and $10,000 on my end. He fought it just to fight. Even though he would tell me constantly that he wanted a divorce and showed how much he hated being married to me, he was pissed I filed for the divorce.

As I was in the middle of the divorce, I began diving into my oldest daughter's sports life. One day, I was talking to her track coach. He was not his usual self, and I asked whether he was okay. He stated that a lot was going on and mentioned he was in the divorce process. At that time, I stayed I understood because I was also going through a divorce, and he was surprised because he knew my husband and stated, "You seem to look like you are happy." My response was, "It is what it looked like." Sadly it was at this point just a show. After that, we continued to talk more due to our situation, leading to us dating several months later. Was it unexpected? Yes. Was it right? Well, it seemed to be okay at the time because both marriages ended. To my understanding, he was already in the divorce process just as I was before our first personal conversation, so I did not feel as if anything was wrong. No, but I stood blinded by my own selfishness, loneliness, and pain because it was dead wrong.

Then more pain came in with the death of my mother, which was hard enough without the big surprise or, let's say, the big family secret. Yea, family secrets again. I tell you secrets can blow up in your face and open up a floodgate of angry, self-destructing pain while trying to continue to protect my brother and my daughter from the truth. I did not want them to feel the pain I was feeling. So I kept it to myself for years, and the anger almost killed me. Because I just did not care anymore, I was like God really. How can you love me so much but cause me this much pain and anger?

If I cannot trust the people close to me and I see them daily, how was I supposed to trust you? So the family secret my mother's family decided to do the obituary, and for some reason, they listed that my brother and I were adopted by my father, which would have been okay if I knew I was adopted. Oh yea, just like that, I find out at thirty-eight that I was adopted. Now I do not know about anyone else, but that just blow up in my gut. I was shocked and that turned to anger and hate toward my family to the point I could not attend my mother's funeral at her home church. The anger of another lie and the fact that someone told me during a time that was convenient for them was more than I could handle. I told my dad I attend one funeral, and I could not go to my mother's hometown to do another mainly because I would not be able to control my rage and look at people that have lied to me my entire life. Was the family upset? Yes, they did not understand why I was so upset when I had a great upbringing. So they called me selfish, spoiled, etc. No one seem to understand that I was upset about the secret that everyone seem to know but me. Again what is important to you is not important to others. At this point in my life, I was really not good for anyone.

But I let this relationship go on for four years; during that time, I can say I truly fell in love with him, a life I did not have during my two marriages. I felt he understood me. I opened up my heart and home to him and all the kids on the track team. My life was a dream come true. I had what I thought was the man, the house that I brought, and the life. I loved what I had, and I excused what I was hearing or the inappropriate phone calls I was getting about his behavior with other women because he knew what I had gone through in the past. I hold a strong belief that he would not do that to me.

But when real life hits, it brings out the true individual all over us. Real life hit when his father was dying, and at the time, I was in real estate, and the market crashed. This is the time when life should bring you together instead of ripping us apart. Emotional, we failed each other. Or let's be real, it was a relationship that started in pain, and it ended in pain. He texted me one day and said, "I couldn't do this anymore," and left.

The ending of this relationship crushed me to the point I was, as I say, unconsciously suicidal. I just existed in a fog. To me, I lost everything, including my home, because I was no longer making money in real estate, so I was losing my income and my home, and I was declaring bankruptcy again. So now bankrupted two kids in college, and the man I loved just walked out of my life. I was living a nightmare. I was able to go back into property management to pay the bills. So daily, I would get up, go to work, and get in my car by the end of the day and emotionally break down.

Then one day, as I was driving home, I had a major panic attack. I would normally drive a back road home with a steep drop at one curb. That day, I realized that I would need to call someone daily for months when I turned onto that road. God opened my mind and heart that day with a panic attack by not letting me be able to get in touch with anyone that day. The fear rushed through me when I saw the curb, the fear that I would turn the steering wheel and run my car off the curb into the steep wooded hill, and all I had at the moment was to call on Jesus to help me.

My mind was out of control. I got home, and the pain hit me so badly like someone had just stabbed me in my heart. I couldn't breathe, and the funny thing was I could not find my cell phone. That was the night that all I had was the Lord. I cried so hard, and the pain was so deep that I truly did not think I would make it through the night. That was the longest night of my life. I felt like I was dying, and honestly, the embarrassment of another relationship failure, losing my home, lost of my finance was killing me, and I did not want to face another day. But, God, I was saved. I woke up the next morning not feeling alone but feeling enough to forgive myself for my mistakes and move forward. Was it easy? No, but it was required.

What did I learn? I learned that to heal your brokenness, you have to accept your mistakes and forgive yourself; if not, it will build up to the point you will consider taking your own life. You will never be at peace or true love with any man. The only physical person that can heal you is you. Once you are ready to heal, God is there to hold you through your worst night and bring you out to the other side. Does it hurt? Oh hell yes, it does. It was the longest and most painful night of my life. And guess what? As much as I knew to be saved, I was pissed. I was mad as hell that He let me go through all that, and I rebelled against God again, but He did not give up on me. He said pretty much do you, but I am not going anywhere, and He didn't. I finally got it, and peace came over me to the point that life was good, and I felt blessed because I was blessed. At the time, did I have materially less than before? Yes, but over-all I had way more. I finally realized that the love of my Lord and Savior was truly unconditional, and it was for me. Now life is amazing. I was loving myself beyond words. But the pressure still continued, and I was still questioning why.

CHAPTER 6

The Pressure of Reality versus the Spiritual Truth

I love this part because your reality will never live up to God's truth. In reality, we want what we want. We make decisions on what and how we are feeling in the season at the moment, which can lead to not asking what God would want us to do. Most of the time, in reality, we are not seeking the voice of God. But it does come to the point in everyone's life that you seek your truth, which can only be answered in the spiritual realm when you truly seek God to lead you.

The reality

The truth is that I could develop hatred for everything that I've gone through. I could hate every person that hurt me. I could have remained angry, mean, disgusting, unloving, and just downright lost, but I noticed that each person I came across in my life was for a reason; each relationship was for a reason. Each man I was in a relationship with was truly a good person in one way or the other. We both did our wrongs, and at the time, we were not the people God intended us to be. I don't take anything away from those relationships because I could not be who I am today. I wish every one of them the best that life can give them.

The other reality is that I was not always there for my daughters. Even though they are wonderful women, they carry the burdens of my decisions during my journey. My oldest daughter has the burden of not trusting others, always expecting them to fail her as I did. She lives with the thought that the only one she can count on is me. This is such a failure on my end because she witnesses me but into men that we're not capable of putting into me.

I was so broken and thought others could help me feel whole to the point that as outspoken as I am, I did not know my worth. My youngest daughter carries the burden of abandonment and rejection as she feels I did. In both cases, I accept that I am the cause of the pain I have caused and understand that they love me through their pain.

I am not saying that I would wish to change anything that happened because I would not be the person I am, and they would not be who they are. I continue to pray for my own forgiveness, and that they find their way through the pain to continue on the journey they now have set for themselves and not let my mistakes cause them to make decisions out of pain.

The spiritual truth

As in Jeremiah 29:11, "'For I know the plans I have for you,' said the Lord. 'They are plans for good and not for disaster, to give you a future and hope.'" God had a plan, He let me stray, but He was always there to keep me by His grace even when I was unlovable, enjoying living in sin, as they say, going to hell and enjoying the trip.

When I was mad and rejected everything I knew about God, He was still there.

But you need to know that His word said for me was in Psalms 37:8–9, "Stop being angry! Turn from your rage! Do not lose your temper—it only leads to harm. For the wicked will be destroyed, but those who trust in the Lord will possess the land." For me, this is saying your anger has caused great harm in your life, as you have read. I was the one that did not trust in the word of God. When I decided that the way things were going was not the actions of a woman that knew that God's grace was over her life. I need to examine myself and go back to what I knew. So I would like to say things changed just like that. No, but things are changing at God's pace, and I am okay with waiting on Him to mold me to be the true woman He created.

CHAPTER 7

God's Plan for the Diamond

When you let go of what you want in your life and decide to go God's way, it is not an easy route the journey is extremely difficult. The journey has so many up and downs because you cannot see what is ahead. You just have to trust in God's word and His plans for you. Once you accept it, then comes the time to live it.

So now there's the preparation for the diamond, more pressure for the shine, and its completion with no apologies.

Preparation

Even when you are deep in your sin, God is preparing you for when you are ready to come out.

Remember, He already knows you, so He is waiting for you to decide to come out of sin.

So for me, I was doing my thing. I was tired, and I was living for myself. I was single, kids in college, financially broke, emotionally broken, mentally drained, alone, and mad that I put so much into people, and now they are all gone. I felt used, abused, and abandoned. So I decided to just do me and now live a more controlled life. See people at a level where there was no substance—a level where no feelings and no emotions were involved. So I started online dating. I figured this would be fun. I could meet people, be whatever and whoever I wanted, and I had complete control.

The funny thing about it was that I did not have control. Because as I was meeting people, I decided that I was behind a computer, so why not just be myself? Be true to me, and see what happens, and that is when God took control. I met several great men, and when I knew God was in, it was when I met my husband. I met several men who were ministers or pastors. I laughed because one said to me that he was putting in his resume for a church and asked whether I wanted him to put in a first lady resume for me. I was like, heck no. I think that was a way of telling me how serious he was about me, which was something I just did not want to hear. Another man asked me to come to church with him. Again, I said no because I thought I would not be a pastor's girlfriend. The idea of being with a pastor or minister was just something that was not on my agenda, not a desire of mine. As a matter of fact, it was outright never to want to be with a pastor.

But the truth is I never thought I would be worthy of being with a true man of God. This is when God stepped and used Facebook to unknowingly introduce us. Yes, Facebook, as we know, God can use anything and anyone to change us or review things or connect people. So in my case, He used Facebook on my forty-eighth birthday to have my future husband see a post I made on a friend's page for him to reach out and just say, "Hi, my name is—," and that he was a friend of James, and "I wanted to wish you a happy birthday." This was a random post, and because I did not want to be rude, I responded on messenger, saying thank you for the birthday wish. That is when I believe God high-fives Himself, saying she made the right decision by responding. Now the plan for my life has started to come to light. This plan really needed some work on my end. God only needed me to accept the plan so that He would work out the rest, and slowly, the cleaning started.

The cleaning

So the cleaning started. I continued to talk to this man that God sent, learning more about just being myself. Now as you can see, it is funny, yes. I talked to a man who happens to be a pastor but continued to just be himself. He made sure that I was clear that being a pastor was what he was called to do, but he was just a man. He was a man that spoke in a manner that left things off the table. What I mean about off the table is he said I made a vow that the next person I would have sex with would be the person I would marry. Well, for me, that was great. I could talk, and that subject would never come up, but I was so elated by that—nothing to get in the mix of getting to know someone. I can say when someone comes to you just as they are, no game, no show, nothing but being themselves like God has said, "Come to me as you are, and He will do the rest." Well, that is what happened. He was himself, which only made it easier to accept me as me.

I can remember all the prayers I was praying to find people in my life that would accept me for me. But I had to realize that I had to accept myself first. I had to accept my mistakes and my lack of faith to move forward in truth.

So we continued to talk daily and then met in person in July, as a matter of fact, Fourth of July weekend. This was, for me, the moment of truth. We hung out on the Fourth of July. Not knowing what to do with him, we drove down to a beach area where I grew up. We got there around 10:00 a.m., parked the car, and just walked and talked. I asked questions and spoke the truth because at this time, I really did not think this would go anywhere, so I just became my corny, blunt, talkative self, and if he had issues, he could leave Virginia and head back to Connecticut because there was nothing to lose. We literally walked and talked until dusk without food, drinks, just conversation, which blew my mind that we were so engulfed in what we had to say that we forgot to eat.

As night was falling and the fireworks were ready to start, we headed back to the car. I remember saying I was unsure where the fireworks would be, but to my amazement, when we got into the car, the fireworks were going off directly in front of us. We had the best seats, and it was amazing to see that God lined it all up. Trees were around us, but the car was facing between the trees in direct view of the fireworks. We could not have asked for a better day or night.

So the cleaning started because all were put out on the table on that great day. I felt peace being with him, and the trust needed to be me. I'll see my faults, mistakes, fears, joys, anger, demons, quirks, and my crazy was out there for him to accept or reject. I was free.

As the weekend ended and he was preparing to head back to Connecticut, he looked at me and said, "Are you in?" And crazy enough, I said I was in. In for what? Only God would know because I never thought I was in for what was coming next. At that moment, we planned for him to come back down in August for an event with my job that was in MD, the Spirit of Baltimore cruise. On that cruise, he asked me to marry him. I said yes, and the journey of change was interesting. People who knew me were so surprised, and they were like, "How long have you known him? When you met, you never spoke of him," and on and on.

"Then how are you going to pack up and leave everything for someone you do not know that well?" The only response I could give them was that I just knew that I had to go, I had to marry him, and it will be just fine. God placed it, and when I told my daughters and advised them that I would be moving to Connecticut in October, all they said was okay, and my older daughter responded with, "Since you are moving, it is time for me also." So she quit her job in September, packed up her things along with half of my house, rented a haul, and left.

Now you wonder whether fear kicked in. No, I call this the time when God put blinders over my eyes. He only let me see forward, not backward, from side to side; He clogged my ears to not hear the negative from people that spoke as if they cared, but I know not all cared. They were more trying to figure out if I was just that crazy. Statements were made that were just uncalled for. But I had one friend that called me and said, "Girl, you have always been crazy. You have been through so much that you will start over again if this does not work out, just as you have in the past. You are a survivor, so go and live your life." That was what I needed at the time.

So October 2014, I left to start my new adventure but not without taking a trip with all my bags packed to take him down to meet my dad and brother. Yea, they met the day I was moving out of Virginia. He asked them for my hand in marriage, and in my dad's way, he said, "Yea, you can have her." But my brother was extra quiet. I know he wanted the best for me, but realizing that this may be the last time seeing me was a little too much for us. But he gave his blessings, and with my blinder on, I stepped out on faith, and I was on my way to a much-unexpected journey.

More pressure for the shine

So now the pressure for the shine begins Truthfully he could have kept that pressure. Think about it; it takes 725,000 pounds per square inch and at a temperature of 2,200 degrees Fahrenheit to create a diamond. Now that is a lot of pressure on a person when God molds you into what He created you to be. He has to remove the worldly mess from you so the spiritual (diamond) can shine bright and be flawless. What I can say is that the pressure is painful.

The pressure will put you in a place that will leave you wondering and then questioning God, saying things like, "You brought me here for this mess. My life was not perfect, but it was okay, and I understood the things around me. I was good. But I listen, and I step out on faith for You to give me this much hate and disrespect." Man, I was mad I was hurt, but I kept the scripture Jeremiah 29:11 in my head.

So let us talk about the pressure in my life that occurred in my new journey. Everything that could go bad outside my marriage happened. My job transfer was two hours one way daily, and my new husband's daughters were not kind. As a matter of fact, they were downright hateful. The church members were not acting like saved people, and then I got a job close to home, where I had to deal with outright racism, got physically assaulted, my father remarried, and my stepmother made Cinderella's story look like a summer vacation. I know and fully believed the devil was trying to kill me again. The hate I received and my experience took me to levels that, for some reason, I never experienced, nor did I think I deserved. My mental and emotional health was at stake. Because people did not know I suffered from an illness and that the stress that they were putting me through could put me in the hospital. But that did not matter because I had to deal with it. I could not give in to the evil around me. I had to be a good wife and a good example because I was now married to a pastor and I did not want him to look bad.

People tried to make me feel unworthy, constantly on the sly. People disrespected me to the point some refused to talk to me at all, and others would not even address me by my name. But you keep going because it will get better. Well, it didn't. As a matter of fact, it has been years, and things are just a little better.

I find myself at a point in my life where no person can accept who you are, and most people cannot handle change. So when God sends change, I say that because God sent me to this life. But people did not accept it, so they tried to destroy me. I know *destroy* is a strong word, just like the word *hate*, but I experienced both with people around me. It reminds me of my vows, "What God has joined together, let no one separate." With this, I realized that not every believer will believe, respect, or honor the work of God. Me being here married to my husband was just that, the work of God.

Then I was told that when you pray for peace, sometimes God will send you everything that will disturb your peace so that you will learn to find your peace in Him. Once I accepted the peace in my mess, God started working more on me. He has given me the strength to speak on my mess, hold my head up, write the book, and walk in the life He has blessed me with and to trust His plans for me. Most of all honor my mess and speak on where He has brought me from.

This is the pressure of understanding that if you are going to do what God created you for, it is going to piss off a lot of people. This is when the devil sliver in and whispers to them to treat you bad, try to destroy your character, and call you outside your name. Try to convince others that you are a person who is despicable and not worthy to know. That is just how it was for me. I was new to the area, and no one wanted to get to know the real me.

I used to get so upset when I would meet someone that knew my husband. They would quickly grab and hug me, and in my ear, they would say, "Don't hurt him." That was my life for the first five years of my marriage. It just got to a point I just stop letting people get that close to me. Why, they did not care. All they wanted to do was make me feel unworthy of being chosen by God for this. So I had to get in my own head talk to God and realize that my presence offended people's insecurity. So I had to walk with my head up. I had to forgive but keep my distance. They already showed me who they are, so there was no reason for me to think any differently and know I had to use my gift from God or some say discernment to know clearly when people are truly sorry for their actions. If they are not, then it is okay. I will continue to walk in my truth, speak my truth, and be grateful that God has used me to speak on His grace and mercy.

Completed with no apologies

There's no apology because everything I did, i.e., every wrong decision I made and the failure I lived through, was necessary for this time. My mistakes are like Girl Scout badges, the war of life wounds. I earned every one of them, and I can proudly display it by speaking on them.

Because I am Sarah, I laughed at God's promise. I am the woman at the well that has been with men that were not mine. I am the woman with the issue of blood. I was dying from the inside and reaching for God's grace for my healing. I am Esther because I had to stand by my beliefs, and I am Ruth because I'm loyal, and I would do all I can for those I love. So don't apologize for how you lived your life. God will use all your good and bad decisions. He will lead you to His plans once you let go. Forgive yourself and thank God for His grace. Remember, He already knew what you were going to do. He let you go through many troubles so He could be there to bring you through.

Let's be real. How often have you fallen to your knees or cried so hard you did not have words? Who did you call when on your knees? And now you sit here and act as if you did nothing. You've always been this way. If anything, you need to apologize for it, the lie you live. Start telling the truth, which is only by the grace of God. You are the woman you are today. Even if you are not being who you should be, you are better than you were.

God already knew what you had done, so just put your head up and walk in His grace by letting Him mold the diamond in you to shine. God will be with you through the process. He was with you on the journey you walked, and He was with you through the pressure to mold you into your diamond shape. All He wants from you now is to just shine, shine, shine, and show His glory.

*Now let's work on your process to be
what God created you to be.*

When the pressure of life, the pressure of your past, come to bring you down, which they will, here are some scriptures. They are words of truth, words of power, and mainly words of salvation. These will help endure the pressure. You do not want the pressure removed because you cannot become who God created you to be. You want to endure and shine on the other end.

The Bible:

When fearful	Psalms 23
Sinned	Psalms 51, 1 John 1
Discouraged	Psalms 34
Disappointed by people	Psalms 27
Guidelines for life	Matthew 5–7, Romans 12
God seems far away	Psalms 139
Seeking peace of mind	Philippians 4:6–8, John 14:27

Let's start by making a commitment to yourself.

I, ______________________________________

__________, am committed to healing myself through accepting my truth. I will be real to myself, accept myself, understand my mistakes, and forgive myself. I am committed to becoming the diamond God created me to be. I will honor myself and my healing.

Loving Me,

____

____

PRAYER FOR HEALING

Dear Lord,

It is me. It is my will to surrender my healing to You and all that I have. I release all control over to You. I release my pain, brokenness, anxiety, and thought of failure. I offer You all that I am so that You may clean my heart. Prepare me for the pressure to become a diamond.

I surrender my past, present, and future issues. My prayer is that You take of my life to lead me in the direction of what You created for me. Lord, speak to me so that I may hear Your precious and holy voice. That I may feel

Your arms wrapped around me on this journey to healing. Lord, close any doors that are not for me and open all doors You have for me. Father, direct me and place my feet in all rooms that glorify You. Heal me, Lord, clean me, Lord. Amen.

Affirmations to continue your healing and your journey.

- I accept all of my journeys.
- I trust me to do what is best for me.
- I forgive myself for not trusting in myself.
- I forgive others for causing me pain, with the understanding they do not have to be in my life.
- I walk in my truth.
- My truth is not someone else truth, and that is fine.
- I will not let people's insecurities affect my confidence.
- I love me enough not to let other people's pain affect me.
- I am devoted to being the best version of myself.
- I will no longer let the fear of my past mistakes affect my life.
- Let go of my fear of disappointment from others
- Let go of saying yes to people. No, will work just fine.

ABOUT THE AUTHOR

Angela D. Elder is the first child of the Most High. She is a wife and a mother blessed with two daughters and two grandchildren. She is what you would say is "real," no fluff. The pressure of life has made her into a woman that has accepted who she is. She has a passion to empower women to not concentrate or be so upset about the pressures of life because it is only here to assist you in stepping into your purpose.